The Pearson Lab Manual for
Developing Writers
Volume C: Essays

Linda Copeland

St. Louis Community College, Meramec

Longman

New York   Boston   San Francisco

London   Toronto   Sydney   Tokyo   Singapore   Madrid

Mexico City   Munich   Paris   Cape Town   Hong Kong   Montreal

The Pearson Lab Manual for Developing Writers: Volume C: Essays

Copyright © 2010 Pearson Education, Inc.

3 4 5 6 7 8 9 10—BRR—12 11

Longman
is an imprint of

www.pearsonhighered.com

ISBN 10:   0 -205-69340-7

ISBN 13: 978-0-205-69340-5

Preface

The Pearson Lab Manual for Developing Writers series has been designed as supplements for any developmental writing text organized along the rhetorical modes. The paragraph and essay workbook exercises illustrate key concepts and encourage students to apply these concepts, which are covered in most writing classes, i.e., audience, topic sentences, thesis statements, coherence, unity, and levels of development. The analysis exercises isolate concepts explained in class and in the primary text and allow students to demonstrate their understanding of these concepts. The building exercises allow students to apply the concepts and provide students with the "raw materials" to develop paragraphs and essays.

For many developmental students, the biggest hurdle to writing is simply coming up with something to say. Some of the paragraph and essay exercises provide much of the information, allowing the students to focus on articulating the main idea and developing organizing strategies. Other writing prompts encourage the students to develop their own ideas through guided prewriting exercises. The revision prompts direct the students' attention to specific key elements of their own writing and to assess whether they have met the needs of their reading audience. Throughout the paragraph and essay workbooks, audience and purpose stay at the forefront of the writing exercises.

The sentence skills workbook provides exercises that apply grammar, punctuation and mechanics rules rather than simply offer skills drills. Composing exercises that highlight specific sentence skills explained in the students' primary text make up most of the exercises. Even those exercises that require students to simply insert a punctuation mark or to choose between two words go further in requiring the student to provide the rationale behind the choices.

What all of the workbooks have in common is that they are built around topics that draw from history, science, popular culture and other areas that not only engage developmental students, but make them feel they are learning in a college-level academic community. The exercises are designed to be challenging, yet engaging and accessible.

Essays Workbook

Table of Contents

Audience and Purpose

Any piece of writing takes on an entirely different style and tone and even content depending upon the audience of readers and what the writer hopes to achieve through the writing—its purpose.

Read each of the following scenarios and complete the writing for the sets of audience and purpose that follow. Feel free to add appropriate details. A few have already been done for you.

1. **You are waiting at a stoplight when your car is hit from behind by an SUV driven by a 68-year-old man who was talking on his cell phone.**

Text message to friends to let them know what happened: My car just got tanked by an old guy trying to talk on a phone! Ugh!

Short narrative of accident for your insurance agent to let him know you weren't at fault:

Email to your parents to let them know you're all right and not at fault:

Personal Experience Paragraph for a Composition Class to show you can tell a brief story that has a point:

I never thought about how much trouble a brief moment of inattention could cause until I was in a car accident. I was on my way to class, going over in my head all of the formulas I would need to remember to do well on the math quiz scheduled for that morning. While I was stopped at a red light, I looked up in my rear view mirror just in time to see a dark red SUV barreling right at me and not slowing down. I had nowhere to go since the intersection ahead of me was filled with the morning traffic. So I planted my foot hard on the brake to keep from getting pushed out into the intersection and waited. Fortunately the driver saw I was stopped and slammed on his own brakes. He still skidded into the back of my car, but the damage could have been much worse. The driver, a 68-year-old man, jumped out of the car and began to apologize profusely. He had simply been talking on the cell phone and not paying attention. As a result of the accident, I missed the math quiz, which lowered my grade in that class. I also missed nearly a week of work while my car was getting fixed, which meant I had to borrow money from my parents to get me through the rest of the month. To make matters worse, my girlfriend nearly broke up with me because I had no car to drive out of town to her school to go with her to the big homecoming football game. This experience taught me the importance of paying attention while I'm driving, so I won't be responsible for bringing so much grief into someone's life.

1

2. **A frayed electrical cord started a fire in the break room where you work. After turning on the fire alarm, you put out the carpet fire with a fire extinguisher. There was some damage to the room, but everyone was evacuated safely from the building.**

Text message to friends to let them know what happened:

Short report to your manager to explain what happened:

On March 14, 2008, I was moving some supplies back to the storage room when I smelled something burning. The smell seemed to be coming from the break room, and when I looked in, I could see the beginnings of flames in the carpet around the electrical outlet. I immediately pushed the fire alarm outside the break room and removed the nearby fire extinguisher. The foam appeared to put out the flames, so I then left the building with the rest of the employees to wait for the fire department. The fire marshal explained that a faulty wire running from the microwave had sparked and caught the carpet on fire. A fifteen inch section of carpet was burned, and there was some damage to the wall. No one was injured.

Short paragraph to include in the company newsletter to inform everyone of the incident:

Short description of what you did as part of your application for a new job. You want to convince the prospective employer that you are level-headed and responsible.

3. **You've just completed your first semester at college, earning a 3.5 GPA. In addition to taking a full load of courses, you worked 20 hours a week.**

Text message to your best friend to share your accomplishment:

Email to your parents who've been worried that you weren't studying enough:

I just got my first grade report today, and I want to put your minds at ease. I totally aced my math and English classes. I got a B in the online math course and even pulled off a B in the psychology class that was giving me so much trouble at the beginning of the semester. Not too bad, right? So having the job while I'm in school isn't such a bad thing as long as my boss lets me take a little time off when I have tests. I'll be coming home this weekend, and we can celebrate one semester down. And, Mom, a supper of your fabulous spaghetti will sure help my brain keep working at full throttle! See you soon!

Note to your boss who has worked with your schedule so you would be able to attend classes:

A brief description of your accomplishment as part of your application to your college's honors program:

Audience Awareness

As part of their application process, job applicants were asked to write about their skills and abilities. Their audience is the employer who will determine whether or not to give them a job.

First, think about the audience. What do you think a prospective employer will want to see in this piece of writing in terms of content, tone and style?

_____

_____

_____

_____

_____

Now read the following excerpts from the job applications and evaluate how well the applicants addressed their audience and achieved their purpose of standing out as the best candidates for the job.

1. I have learned to multi-task at my current job at a video rental store. I can straighten shelves, wait on customers, take phone orders, and update inventory orders and still have time to work on my homework for my college classes.

What does this writer do well to reach the audience and achieve her purpose?

_____

_____

_____

What could the writer do to better impress her audience and achieve her purpose?

_____

_____

_____

4

2. I communicate well with other people. I am doing very well in my english and communications classes. I was also one of ten students picked to be conflict mediators for other students who where having conflicts with there peers or sometimes even there teachers.

What does this writer do well to reach the audience and achieve his purpose?

_____
_____
_____

What could the writer do to better impress the audience and achieve his purpose?

_____
_____
_____

3. At my last job in a retail department store, I started as a sales assistant and earned five customer services awards. Then I was promoted to a customer service specialist. Working for your company would allow me to continue to increase my earning potential.

What does this writer do well to reach the audience and achieve his purpose?

_____
_____
_____

What could the writer do to better impress the audience and achieve his purpose?

_____
_____
_____

4. I am a dependable person cause I show up to work and on time every day. Sometimes I stay late just so I can finish my work.

What does this writer do well to reach the audience and achieve her purpose?

_____
_____
_____

What could the writer do to better impress her audience and achieve her purpose?

_____
_____
_____

The Thesis Statement

Just as a topic sentence presents the subject and controlling idea of a paragraph, the thesis presents the subject and controlling idea of an essay. Like a topic sentence, the thesis should present the writer's point. It should take a stand or present an opinion about the subject.

Identify each of the following as an announcement (A), too broad (B), too narrow (N) or a thesis statement (T).

____ There are many problems with computers.
____ This essay will discuss the dangers of computer viruses.
____ You can take some simple precautions to protect your computer from viruses.
____ If your computer makes unusual sounds or randomly plays music, it may have a virus.

____ As gas prices continue to rise, the unique Aptera may soon be the vehicle of choice for many Americans.
____ The Aptera prototype gets 230 miles per gallon of gas, but the manufacturer is aiming for over 300 miles per gallon.
____ I want to convince you to buy an Aptera.
____ The high price of gasoline has greatly impacted the United States.

____ In 1868 Thomas Henry Huxley first suggested birds and reptiles had a common ancestor.
____ Strong evidence supports the theory that birds evolved from dinosaurs.
____ Fossils can teach us many things about the past.
____ In this paper I will show how birds may have evolved from dinosaurs.

____ The Cardiff Giant hoax of 1869 captured headlines with its controversies.
____ People have enjoyed hoaxes for centuries.
____ Let's look at how hoaxes trick people.
____ The famous showman P.T. Barnum joined in the Cardiff Giant Hoax.

____ *Godzilla* is one of the most famous monster films of the 1950's.
____ My essay will compare the American version of *Godzilla* with the Japanese version.
____ For the Japanese, the original *Godzilla* was a high quality film with a powerful message.
____ Movies say a lot about the time and culture in which they are made.

____ Environment plays an important role in our lives.
____ Some simple changes in your workplace environment can greatly reduce stress.
____ Poor lighting can cause workplace stress.
____ Here are the ways you can reduce stress in the workplace.

*For more practice with **the thesis statement**, go to www.mywritinglab.com... MyWritingLab...**where better practice makes better writers!***

Essay Unity

The topic sentence of each body paragraph in an essay must support the thesis statement. In each of the following sets, circle the letter of the topic sentence that does not support the thesis statement.

1. Thesis: Participation in extracurricular clubs and activities is an important part of the college experience.
    a. Some organizations will allow you to practice skills needed for your target career.
    b. Getting overextended through too many commitments to organizations can cause your grades to suffer.
    c. Joining organizations can be a way to meet others who share your interests.
    d. Holding office in an organization will show future employers that you have leadership skills.

2. Thesis: New managers often make some basic mistakes in their leadership roles.
    a. New managers may confuse discipline with punishment in dealing with employees.
    b. New managers may feel dependent upon employees and tolerate inadequate work performance.
    c. New managers may feel sorry for employees and become too understanding of poor performance.
    d. New managers can benefit from a mentor program that matches them with a higher level administrator.

3. Thesis: Because living together is not the same as "hanging out," best friends need to take steps to assure a successful relationship as roommates.
    a. Best friends need to accept that people change and learn to adapt.
    b. Friends should establish some ground rules before moving in together.
    c. Sharing an apartment is more stressful and demanding than sharing a dorm room.
    d. Best friends should be prepared for stress and how to handle it constructively.

4. Thesis: Successful employees know how to balance their personal and professional lives.
    a. College internships can provide you important on-the-job training that classroom work cannot duplicate.
    b. Sharing too many personal details of your life at work can negatively affect your professional reputation.
    c. Not sharing anything about your personal life may keep your fellow employees from feeling connected to you.
    d. There are some basic guidelines to follow when discussing your personal life at the office.

8

Organizing Details into Unified Paragraphs

Complete the following outline for an essay by placing the supporting details under the main points they best support. Some details will not be used.

Thesis Statement: The reasons behind the nicknames of our states are as diverse as the states themselves.

I. Some nicknames recall significant events within a state's history.

A. _____

B. _____

C. _____

D. _____

E. _____

II. Distinctive geographical features are another source of nicknames.

A. _____

B. _____

C. _____

D. _____

III. Some states base their nicknames on what grows well in the native soil.

A. _____

B. _____

C. _____

D. _____

Illinois, the "Prairie State" takes pride in celebrating and preserving its sweeping prairies.

Kansas took its nickname the "Sunflower State," from the wild flowers that dotted its expansive plains.

Another state that chose its nickname based upon having a "first" is Wyoming, known as the "Equality State" for being the first to give women the right to vote, to hold public office and to serve on juries.

The bluish-purple buds of its native grass gave Kentucky the nickname the "Bluegrass State."

California took the nickname the "Golden State" because its development was spurred by the discovery of gold in 1848.

Missouri proudly calls itself the "Show-Me State," a nickname that acknowledges common sense as well as stubbornness.

Great forests of native evergreens gave nicknames to two states: Maine, the "Pine Tree State" and Washington, the "Evergreen State."

Iowa is known as the "Hawkeye State" in honor of Chief Black Hawk.

Delaware laid claim to the nickname "First State" since in 1787, it was the first state to ratify the U.S. Constitution.

Arizona, of course, calls itself the "Grand Canyon State."

The "Buckeye State," Ohio took its nickname from the many buckeye trees that once thrived there.

While not the first to sign the U.S. Constitution, Connecticut took the nickname the "Constitution State" because some historians claim that the first constitution in history was written there.

With borders touching four of the five Great Lakes, Michigan calls itself the "Great Lakes State."

Oregon took the name the "Beaver State" in honor of one of its native animals, which had been hunted to near extinction before protective measures re-established its presence in the state's rivers and streams.

Perhaps because it couldn't choose just one of its geographical features or part of its natural beauty to celebrate, Arkansas is known as the "Natural State."

Because the volunteer soldiers from Tennessee served with distinction under General Andrew Jackson at the Battle of New Orleans during the War of 1812, Tennessee is known as the "Volunteer State."

Developing an Essay with Supporting Examples and Details I

The following essay lacks supporting examples and details in the body paragraphs. Drawing from your own experiences and observations, add the support that will add interest and clarity to this essay.

Most people want to live long and healthy lives free from illness and aches and pains. In the course of daily life, however, it's easy to fall into bad habits and behaviors that make getting sick likely or even inevitable.

A common route on the road to poor health is a careless diet. Some people simply avoid nutritious foods that contain important vitamins. _____
_____
_____
_____

Then there are those who set themselves up for health problems by eating too much of the wrong kinds of foods. _____
_____
_____
_____

Poor diets such as these can cause a number of health problems. _____
_____
_____
_____

In addition to diet, people's level of activity plays a role in their health. A lack of exercise can certainly contribute to an unhealthy future, and many people's daily lives contain almost no physical activity. _____
_____
_____

These sedentary lifestyles can eventually lead to several health problems. _____
_____
_____

On the other hand, some people can engage in too much physical activity. _____
_____
_____

Excessive and repeated strain on the body also has a negative impact on health. _____
_____
_____
_____

Perhaps most surprising are the people who engage in activities that everyone knows will have serious health consequences. For example, _____
_____
_____

This can lead to _____
_____
_____

There are also those who _____
_____
_____

The negative consequences of this include _____
_____
_____

Finally, some people actually _____
despite repeated warnings from medical authorities. _____
_____
_____

It's nearly inevitable that this will have a serious impact on their health. _____
_____
_____
_____

Life certainly is a lot more enjoyable with good health, yet many people continue to lead lifestyles that are sure to cause them health problems sooner or later. In *Book of Comforts*, Patricia Alexander writes, "The people who say they don't have time to take care of themselves will soon discover they're spending all their time being sick." I, for one, agree with her.

12

Developing an Essay with Supporting Examples and Details II

The following essay lacks supporting examples and details in the body paragraphs. Drawing from your own experiences and observations, add the support that will add interest and clarity to this essay.

During tough economic times, life can be less stressful if you can learn to cut back on spending. At the same time, you don't want to give up having fun and enjoying life. There are ways to both save money and have fun if you exercise a little creativity.

If you enjoy shopping, you don't have to go to the high end stores at the mall to find lots of bargains. Some stores carry quality products at affordable prices. For example, _____

_____

_____

_____

Also, consider online shopping as a way to save money. _____

_____

_____

_____

Remember, too, that quality products do not always have to be bought brand new. _____

_____

_____

_____

_____

If, in addition to shopping, you enjoy going out to eat, your love of fine food doesn't have to end when you tighten your belt. Cooking your own food rather than going out to restaurants can have several advantages that save you money. _____

_____

_____

_____

You can also save money at the grocery store when you shop for the ingredients for those home-cooked meals. _____

_____

_____

_____

_____

_____

13

Even entertainment does not have to end because money is tight. Going to the movies, for instance, can cost you $20 or more for tickets along with a drink and snack. You can have just as much fun more affordably by inviting a few friends over for a movie night at your house.

_____
_____
_____
_____

You can do something similar for sporting events if tickets for the live professional events are out of your budget's range. _____

_____
_____
_____

A romantic date can also be put together on a shoestring budget. _____

_____
_____
_____
_____

You can stay healthy financially and still enjoy life to the fullest, and, who knows, you may actually enjoy your budget-conscious lifestyle more than your wild days of free-spending. Having the best of both worlds—a good time and money in your pocket—may be hard to give up.

*For more practice with **recognizing, developing, and organizing an essay**, go to www.mywritinglab.com... MyWritingLab...**where better practice makes better writers!***

Expanding a Cause and Effect Paragraph into an Essay

Like paragraphs, essays are unified and coherent. The biggest difference is that an essay can more fully develop a topic. Read the following paragraph about the reasons people are fired from their jobs. Then follow the prompts for expanding this paragraph into an essay.

Getting fired often involves ignoring some basic expectations. Employers expect their employees to know how to do the work they were hired to do. Those employees who overstated their experience or qualifications during a job interview may find themselves fired if they cannot quickly learn their jobs. Similarly, frustrated employers will fire those who work too slowly and make frequent errors. Employers also expect employees to get along with their colleagues. While some people have more social skills than others, all employees can show respect towards their co-workers. Most employers will not tolerate employees who spread malicious gossip, blame colleagues for problems, and behave rudely toward others. Perhaps the most important expectation employers have is honesty. Employees who falsify time sheets, expense reports and project reports nearly always face termination when they are caught. Stealing company materials and equipment is grounds for dismissal as well as using company resources and time for non-company business. Employers expect employees to be qualified, personable and honest. Someone not meeting these expectations will soon hear the dreaded words, "You're fired!"

1. First, determine the topic sentence and main idea sentences. Those will become the basis for thesis statement and topic sentences in your essay.

Topic Sentence: _____
_____

Main Idea #1 _____
_____

Main Idea #2 _____
_____

Main Idea #3_____
_____

15

2. Next, you need to brainstorm some more details and examples to expand and clarify the main points from the paragraph. Also, in the course of brainstorming, you may come up with another main idea or two that you could use in another paragraph in your essay. Remember, essays are not limited to only three body paragraphs. Here are some ideas to get you started.

using work time for personal business ignoring safety rules
inappropriate dress acting like a know-it-all
playing games on Internet during work coming to work hung over or intoxicated
showing up late and/or leaving early repeatedly inappropriate emails
constantly complaining bringing personal life to work

_____
_____
_____
_____
_____
_____
_____
_____
_____
_____

Remember: Specific examples <u>show</u> what you mean. Examples lend clarity and interest to your writing. Draw from your own observations of workplace behaviors.

3. Now organize the main points you will develop in a short essay. Each main point will be developed into a paragraph. Include under each main point the kinds of supporting details (SD below) you will use to develop it. Like the paragraph, you may have three main points, or you may have come up with another as a result of your brainstorming.

Thesis: _____
_____

I. _____
 SD_____
 SD_____
 SD_____
 SD_____

II. _____
 SD_____
 SD_____
 SD_____
 SD_____

III. _____
 SD_____
 SD_____
 SD_____
 SD_____

IV. _____

    SD_____

    SD_____

    SD_____

    SD_____

4. Write a first draft of your essay about getting fired.

5. Revise your draft.

You can make your introduction more lively and engaging for your readers in several ways.

    a. Begin with an interesting story or example. Are there any of the examples you generated during brainstorming that you think would make a good opening to this essay?

    b. Begin with a quote. Here are some quotes about getting fired. Do any of these fit the point you want your essay to make?

> "You never ask why you've been fired because if you do, they're liable to tell you."
> Jerry Coleman
>
> "Most people work just hard enough not to get fired and get paid just enough money not to quit."
> George Carlin
>
> "If you aren't *fired* with enthusiasm, you will be *fired* with enthusiasm. "
> Vince Lombardi

    c. Begin with a fact or a surprising statistic.

How have you revised your introduction?_____

_____

_____

Why do you think this is better?_____

_____

_____

Unity Check each body paragraph to make sure it has a clear topic sentence that lets the reader know the subject and controlling idea of the paragraph. Do all the topic sentences support the thesis statement? Make sure all the sentences in each paragraph support its controlling idea.

What have you done to improve the unity of your essay?_____

_____

_____

_____

_____

Coherence How have you organized the paragraphs in this essay? Did you consider using an emphatic organization—least to most important reason? Have you used transitions to connect each body paragraph in your essay? Look for ways to improve the transitions between paragraphs. Don't settle for using only simple, one-word transitions like "First," "Next" and "Álso." Check the coherence of each individual paragraph as well. The paragraphs should have a clear organization and varied transitions. Avoid simply "listing" the examples in your paragraphs.

What have you done to improve the coherence of this essay?_____
_____
_____
_____
_____

Development Do you have enough specific support in each paragraph? If you have short three and four sentence paragraphs, can you compose a topic sentence that would allow you to combine them? Or what information do you need to further develop the weak paragraphs?
What have you done to improve the development of this essay?_____
_____
_____
_____
_____

Edit the revised essay.

*For more practice with **cause and effect**, go to www.mywritinglab.com... MyWritingLab...**where better practice makes better writers!***

Building a Description Essay

Imagine that the owners of a house or apartment—your own or one that you know well—are planning to spend a year abroad and want to find someone willing to rent their fully furnished home while they're gone. They have asked you to write a short essay describing their home in a positive way that will attract someone willing to rent it for a year.

Step #1 Mapping and Brainstorming

Use the following map to generate specific details about the home. Parts have been completed for you. Make whatever additions or changes you need to fit the home you are describing. For example, the home may have a finished basement or a wrap-around porch. The apartment complex may have a gated security system and a pool. Instead of a yard, the apartment may be close to a park.

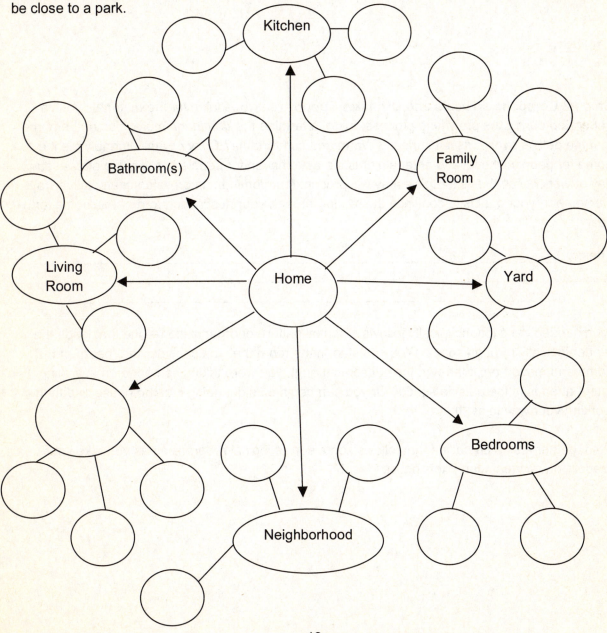

After you have used mapping to come up with the main features of the home, brainstorm some specific details about each feature. Try to use words that will evoke your readers' senses in a positive way. You want your readers to be able to visualize this home and to feel its comforts.

Step #2 Compose a Thesis and Organize Support As you look over the materials you've generated during the prewriting process, try to determine the *dominant impression* of the home that the details evoke. Is it luxurious? Warm and comfortable? Cozy? Family friendly? Is it a home for people who love to entertain or is it a quiet haven for people to retreat to after a long day at work? The thesis for this essay will present that dominant impression in a positive way. Remember, your goal is to convince the reader through your description to rent this home for a year.

Thesis: _____
_____
_____

An extended description typically follows a spatial pattern of organization—one that leads the reader logically through space. You can start in the room that you consider the "heart" of the home and move from it through the house as though you were taking someone on a walking tour that ends in the outside space. Or you can begin outside, going into the house and then working your way to its "heart."

Put together a scratch outline that follows some sort of logical progression as you take your readers on a virtual tour of this house.

Step #3—Drafting   Write a first draft of this essay.

Step #4—Analyze the Draft for Revision and Revise

1. It would be logical to begin this essay by giving some explanation of the circumstances behind this house—the family leaving for a year and so on. But at the same time, you want to have a hook to catch the reader's interest. What "hook" do you use in this introduction? If your first draft does not have a hook, what might you do in the revision?

2. Look at the overall organization you have used in this essay. Does it move logically through space from beginning to end? What strategy did you use in organizing the details into separate paragraphs? How did you avoid having one long paragraph or too many short choppy paragraphs?

3. Looking further at the organization, give examples of some of the transitions you used to move your readers through the space both inside and outside of the house.

4. As you describe this house, you do not want your details to seem random. You want them to all work together to create the dominant impression of the house that you presented in your thesis. Give examples of some of the details you use throughout the description to support this dominant impression.

Dominant Impression: _____

Supporting Details: _____
                      _____
                      _____
                      _____
                      _____
                      _____
                      _____
                      _____
                      _____

5. What do you do in the conclusion to bring the description to a clear end and to encourage the readers to consider renting this home?

6. Based on your responses to these questions, what changes do you plan to make as you revise this essay?

Step #5 Edit Revised Draft

*For more practice with **description**, go to www.mywritinglab.com... MyWritingLab...**where better practice makes better writers!***

Analyzing a Narrative Essay

Carefully read the following narrative essay and answer the questions that follow.

Floyd Collins, the son of a poor farmer, grew up exploring caves in the region of Kentucky long famous for its fabulous caverns. Crystal Cave, located on the Collins' farm, had exceptionally beautiful crystal formations, but attracted few tourists because the cave was so far from the main road leading to popular and profitable Mammoth Cave. Hoping to find another entrance to Mammoth Cave or a new cave closer to the tourists' route, Floyd began exploring other caves in the region and soon found what he thought was a promising venture in Sand Cave. On Friday, January 30, 1925, Floyd was crawling out through a narrow passage in Sand Cave when he dislodged a rock from the ceiling, pinning his leg and trapping him.

When family and friends found Floyd the next morning, they tried everything they could to get him out, but Floyd was stuck tight. By Monday morning, newspapers around the country had picked up the story, and soon the relatively new media of radio was broadcasting regular updates of the rescue efforts. Firefighters, geologists, stone masons and mining experts arrived with advice on how to rescue Floyd. A college president offered to send in his basketball team to dig Floyd out, and an heiress from Chicago offered to send her surgeon to amputate Floyd's leg. Eventually, there were over three hundred volunteer rescuers, fifty reporters from newspapers all over the country, and nearly twenty thousand spectators on hand for the Sand Cave rescue. Even vendors appeared, selling food, drinks and souvenirs to the crowds.

While the would-be rescuers were able to reach Floyd to give him some milk and juice, they made no progress towards freeing him from the tunnel. At one point, Skeets Miller, a young reporter from a Louisville newspaper, squeezed down the tunnel and interviewed the weakening Floyd. While the interview did little to help Floyd, Miller later won the Pulitzer Prize for his daring reporting of the story. Shortly after Miller's interviews, the tunnel above Floyd collapsed, completely cutting him off from the outside. Rescuers began digging a shaft to try to reach Floyd, and finally on February 16, they found the unlucky cave explorer dead from starvation and exposure.

Today, the historical marker outside Sand Cave says that Floyd's story "Aroused the sympathy of a nation." Was it sympathy that made Floyd's story one of the biggest news events of the time, or simply morbid curiosity fueled by an aggressive news media? Whatever caused it, the fascination with Floyd's ordeal continued long after his death, inspiring books, a movie, a documentary and even a musical. Floyd went into Sand Cave a poor Kentucky backwoodsman and emerged a folk hero.

1. The introduction of a narrative essay often answers the same questions as the opening paragraph of a good newspaper story: Who? What? When? Where? Why? Look over the introduction paragraph and see if it gives you the answers to the following questions.

Who is this story about? _____

When does this story take place? _____

Where does this story take place? _____

What happens in this story? _____

_____

Why did this happen? _____

_____

2. What in this introduction makes readers curious and want to read on?

3. What do the details in the first body paragraph suggest to you about the rescue attempt? How well planned was it? What seems to be the priority of the people gathered outside Sand Cave?

4. What kind of organization pattern does this essay follow? Give examples of some of the transitions the writer uses throughout the essay.

5. The Sand Cave rescue was one of the biggest news stories of its time. Why do you think so many people were fascinated by this drama as it played out? Why do you think this story continued to fascinate people for decades after it happened?

6. The writer of this narrative does not explicitly state the point of the story, and there are several possible. What do you think is the main point of this essay? What are some other possible lessons?

7. Sometimes the writer of a short narrative must make hard decisions about what details to include or not include. The following are additional details about Floyd Collins' story that the writer might have included. Put the letter of the detail where you think it would best fit in the essay. Cross out details you would not include.

a. Floyd's body was left in the tunnel, and the family held a funeral service at the surface.

b. Floyd's own father worked the crowds during the rescue, posing for photographs and handing out flyers promoting Crystal Cave.

c. It cost $1 to enter Mammoth Cave and $4 to stay all day.

d. Skeet Miller fed Floyd milk through a rubber hose and tried unsuccessfully to lift the rock off with a jack.

e. In April Floyd's family retrieved his body from the cave and buried him near crystal cave.

f. Doctors estimated that Floyd died sometime between February 12 and February 16.

g. Floyd was trapped 125 feet below ground in a space 8 inches high and 12 feet long.

h. Floyd discovered Crystal Cave on his father's farm when he chased a ground hog down a hole.

i. After Floyd's family sold Crystal Cave, the new owners moved Floyd's body to a glass-topped coffin and exhibited it in Crystal Cave until vandals stole the body in 1929.

j. The Louisville newspaper described Skeet Miller as a hero.

k. The boulder that wedged against Floyd's leg weighed less than 27 pounds.

l. At one point, rescuers tried to pull Floyd out with a harness.

m. When Floyd's stolen body was found, with its left leg missing and never recovered, it was returned to the glass-topped coffin, which was chained and kept in a secluded part of Crystal Cave.

n. The Kentucky governor sent in two detachments of soldiers to maintain order, and the Red Cross set up a field hospital outside Sand Cave.

o. When Floyd's family could not free him, they offered a $500 reward for his rescue.

p. In 1961, the Mammoth Cave National Park System bought and closed Crystal Cave, and at his family's request, Floyd's body was finally buried in a local cemetery in 1989.

q. Floyd went into the cave alone without proper clothing or equipment, which was very foolish.

Introduction paragraph

First body paragraph

Second body paragraph

A new third body paragraph

Conclusion paragraph

25

Building a Narrative Essay

Write a narrative essay about a time you helped someone or were yourself helped by others. Your readers for this essay are your peers who would enjoy reading a lively story that helps them better understand human nature.

Step #1 Brainstorming and Freewriting on the Journalist's Questions

First, brainstorm some possible situations you can write about in a short essay. Try to come up with four to six possible subjects—times you helped someone—by yourself or with others—or times you were helped.

_____

_____

_____

_____

_____

_____

A good narrative must have a point. It should teach us or help us better understand something about what it means to be a human being. In the narrative about Floyd Collins, for example, one point could be that people motivated by money may take unnecessary risks. Another could be how the power of the media can stir up people's interest in an event. Another point of the story could deal with people's morbid fascination with tragedy.

Look over your possible subjects. Which one best lends itself to a story that makes a point about needing help or giving help? Which could best give insights into how and why people behave the way they do?

Once you have a topic, use the journalist's questions to generate through freewriting details to use in your narrative.

Who are the people in the story?_____

_____

_____

_____

_____

Where and when does the story take place? _____

_____

_____

_____

What is the problem or conflict in the story that must be resolved? _____

_____

_____

26

How is the conflict resolved? _____
_____
_____
_____

Step #2 Compose a Thesis and Organize Support   Although you may not even present your thesis statement explicitly in your essay, you should have a working thesis to keep you focused on the point you want your narrative to make. Having a focused point makes it a little easier to decide which details are most relevant and should be included and which details should be left out. Here are ways the author of the Floyd Collins essay might have presented the point in an explicit thesis:

The Sand Cave rescue of Floyd Collins shows the American public's fascination with tragedy. Taking dangerous risks to make money led to tragedy for Floyd Collins.

Compose a working thesis that presents the main point you want your narrative to make.

Thesis: _____
_____
_____

A narrative follows a chronological order, so you will present the events of the story as they occur in time. The challenge is how to group these events in paragraphs, since you will not have topic sentences like you do in writing that explains or persuades.

For a short narrative, you might consider using the following plan to group or cluster the details of the story.

    I.   Background (What led up to the problem requiring help?)
   II. The actual problem
   III. The resolution of the problem

You'll need to decide if you can present the background information in the introduction paragraph—as was done in the Floyd Collins essay—or in the first body paragraph.

Write a short scratch outline for your essay, including what will be covered in each section.

Step #3—Drafting   Write a first draft of this essay.

Step #4—Analyze the Draft for Revision and Revise

1. What do you do in your introduction to generate the readers' interest in this narrative? What might you also do to create a sense of suspense?

2. Do you state your thesis explicitly or is it implied (not stated directly)? If it is explicit, where does it appear? The introduction? The conclusion?   If it is implied, what have you done to make sure the reader understands the point of this story?

3. Look at how you have broken your narrative into paragraphs. What was the logic you used in breaking your story down into paragraphs?

4. Give examples of some of the transitions you used to move your readers through the time frame of your story. What else can you do to improve the coherence or flow of the story for the reader?

5. Give at least four examples of details you used in the story to make the situation vivid for the readers.

6. What details have you used that may not be particularly relevant in shaping the point of the story? Consider taking these details out and adding more details relevant to getting your point across.

28

7. How does your conclusion wrap up the narrative? Put yourself in the place of a reader who knows nothing about the situation you have described. Do you notice any "loose ends" or questions that readers may still have?

8. Based on your answers to these questions, what revisions do you plan to make?

Step #5 Edit Final Draft

*For more practice with **narration**, go to www.mywritinglab.com... MyWritingLab...**where better practice makes better writers!***

Building an Illustration Essay

      An illustration essay supports its point primarily through illustrations or examples. Add your own ideas to the following materials to build an illustration essay about superstitions in sports.

Step #1 Brainstorming Here are some examples of superstitions in professional sports. Brainstorming alone or with classmates, add to this list any sports superstitions you know. Include your own superstitions if you play sports or those of people you know.

Hockey players don't leave sticks crossed—bad luck
bouncing ball before a foul shot—good luck in basketball
NASCAR drivers avoid green cars—first racing accident to kill two drivers—one drove green car
Wade Boggs—ate chicken before every game for good luck called "Chicken Man"
Baseball players step on at least one of the bases when running off field-- good luck
bad luck to touch one of the baselines while running on or off the field between innings
peanut shells around a race car—bad luck never eat peanuts before a race
good luck—tap goalie on shin pads before a hockey game
Michael Jordan always wore his North Carolina Tarheel shorts underneath his game shorts.
Hockey players don't shave until their team is eliminated from playoffs
good luck—be last player to throw a basket during warm-ups
While rookie with Montreal Canadians, goalie Patrick Roy would talk to goal posts before games
before every game Roy skates to blue line—<u>never</u> steps on it, envisions goal net shrinking
Sterling Marlin eats a bologna sandwich before every NASCAR race—good luck
Point guard Daryl Armstrong won't cut off goatee—luck to avoid injury
bad luck to mention no-hitter to the pitcher during the game
Turk Wendell, relief pitcher, chewed licorice and brushed teeth between innings

_____
_____
_____
_____
_____
_____
_____
_____
_____
_____

Now brainstorm reasons you think people—especially athletes—might be superstitious.

_____
_____
_____
_____
_____

Step #2 Organizing

Think about the point you want this essay to make about superstitions in sports. What new insights or understanding do these examples give you? What would you like the reader to better understand about superstition?

_____
_____
_____
_____
_____

Use these ideas and the ideas generated through brainstorming to write a tentative thesis statement for this essay:

Thesis:_____
_____
_____

Now, organize your examples into body paragraphs. What are some logical ways you can group or cluster your examples? Remember, each body paragraph will have a topic sentence that makes a point about your thesis.

TS:_____
_____
_____
_____
_____

TS:_____
_____
_____
_____

TS:_____
_____
_____
_____

TS:_____
_____
_____
_____

31

Step #3 Drafting Write a rough draft of this illustration essay.

Step #4 Revising

1. You can make your introduction more lively and engaging for your readers in several ways.

    d. Begin with an interesting story or example. Are there any examples you generated during brainstorming that you think would make a good opening to this essay?

    e. Begin with a quote. Here are some quotes about superstitions. Do any of them fit the point you want your essay to make?

    > "I had only one superstition. I made sure to touch all the bases when I hit a home run."
    > Babe Ruth
    >
    > "Superstition is foolish, childish, primitive and irrational -- but how much does it cost you to knock on wood?" Judith Viorst, *Love, Guilt & the Meaning of Life, Etc.*
    >
    > "Superstitions are habits rather than beliefs." –Marlene Dietrich

    f. Begin with a fact or a surprising statistic.

    How have you revised your introduction?_____
    _____
    _____
    Why do you think this is better?_____
    _____
    _____

2. **Unity** Check each body paragraph to make sure it has a clear topic sentence that lets the reader know the subject and controlling idea of the paragraph. Do all the topic sentences support the thesis statement? Make sure all the sentences in each paragraph support its controlling idea.
    What have you done to improve the unity of your essay?_____
    _____
    _____
    _____
    _____

3. **Coherence** Have you used transitions to connect each body paragraph in your essay? Look for ways to improve the transitions between paragraphs. Don't settle for using only simple, one-word transitions like "First," "Next" and "Also." Check the coherence of each individual paragraph as well. The paragraphs should have a clear organization and varied transitions. Avoid simply "listing" the examples in your paragraphs.

What have you done to improve the coherence of this essay?_____

_____

_____

_____

_____

4. **Development**   Do you have enough specific support in each paragraph? If you have short, three and four sentence paragraphs, can you compose a topic sentence that would allow you to combine them? What information do you need to further develop the weak paragraphs?

    What have you done to improve the development of this essay?_____

    _____

    _____

    _____

    _____

Step #5 Edit Revised Draft

For more practice with **illustration**, *go to* www.mywritinglab.com... *MyWritingLab...****where better practice makes better writers!***

Analyzing a Classification Essay

The following draft of a classification essay has been marked up by the instructor. Revise and edit the essay according to the instructor's suggestions.

> The essay needs a more engaging title.

Classifying Homework Assignments

> Can you find a way to avoid this cliché?

Throughout their academic careers, students will have to deal with homework. For those who pursue higher education, the homework bar is set at new heights. Few and far between are those classes that don't require hours of outside homework that cut into time that could be spent earning money to pay for more classes or just relaxing with friends and family. However, not all homework is created equal. Homework assignments can range from mind-numbing wastes of time to truly engaging learning experiences.

> Check punctuation. You have two errors in this sentence.

Students are most frustrated by the homework they think is a waste of their time. These assignments do not clearly connect to the goals of the class nor do they engage the students interest. For example, I once had a composition teacher who assigned a list of 100 trivia questions for the class to answer by using only print sources in the library. After more than eight hours of library work, I knew

> Can you briefly tell why this assignment would have been better?

such facts as when the Mongols first invaded China and the depth of Crater Lake in California. An hour tour of the library before a research paper assignment would have been more practical and helpful. A psychology teacher required each

> A transition would make this next example seem less abrupt.

student to read ten outside articles that dealt with any kind of "social interaction" and write up a one page summary of each article. Each summary earned a

> You unnecessarily shift person here.

checkmark at the top and ten points but, while easy to complete, did little to help anyone better understand what was covered in the rest of the course. Rather than

> Check this paragraph for unity. There are two sentences where you get a bit off track. Cross them out.

helping students learn, these kinds of assignments are more like little hurdles for us to overcome in order to pass a class.

A little less frustrating are those assignments that meet the goals of the class but do not excite or interest the students. Long reading assignments in history, for instance, are often boring to get through, but if the material helps students better understand things and do well on tests, the assignment is

> This is a weak word. Can you find a more precise one?

tolerable. Working through twenty algebra equations may be the kind of practice that leads to a perfect score on a test, but for some students, ten practice

34

equations would do the trick. I'm not even a math major, and I can understand how to do an equation after solving four or five. Composition teachers often assign topics for papers that hold no interest whatsoever for students. These assignments probably teach something about writing, but they are such a chore to write that students sometimes do poorly because they are bored or frustrated by them. Students can better tolerate these kinds of assignments that may help them understand the course material because certain required classes have to be passed whether they interest students or not. I, for example, have three more general education classes to complete, and then I can focus on classes in my major, which is horticulture.

A transition or two may help coherence in this part of your paragraph.

Thankfully, there are those homework assignments that catch students up in the excitement of learning. For example, I once had a business teacher who gave us case studies involving typical problems encountered in the business world that students had to solve. Not only did completing these case studies help me better understand the business concepts covered on the exam, but the interesting and real world problems gave helpful insights into what I might encounter in a business career. These case studies were practical and even fun to work on, and I found that homework to be some of the best of my college career. Assignments that are kind of different and teach useful information make students want to learn.

You have only one example here. You need another example or two in order to "show" the reader what kinds of assignments are exciting.

"Kind of different"? Can you be more precise here?

It's likely homework will always take up a good chunk of a college student's life. Also, it's not likely that every assignment will please him or her. However, teachers can make homework a more rewarding experience for most students by making sure it relates to the class and when possible, adding a little extra fun and excitement to the homework mix.

Use plurals consistently to avoid the wordy "him or her" constructions.

Again, the reader will better understand what you mean here if you include more examples of these kinds of assignments in your last body paragraph.

Building a Classification Essay

You've examined a classification essay that classifies the kinds of assignments students encounter in their college classes. As a college student, you probably could relate to what the writer was saying. Now, using your experience as a college student, write an essay that classifies some element of college life for readers who may not be so familiar with the subject. Imagine your readers are students who are just beginning their first semester and have no idea what to expect about their classes, their teachers, fellow students or any other part of the college experience.   Possible subjects include the following:

kinds of students one encounters in group work
kinds of excuses for missing class or not turning in assignments
kinds of classroom participation
kinds of lecture styles
kinds of lab partners

Brainstorm some other subjects that lend themselves to a classification of three or four categories.

_____
_____
_____

Step #1 Brainstorming Once you have determined a subject, brainstorm some ways you can classify your subject into categories.

_____
_____
_____
_____

Once you have three or four categories, brainstorm some examples and descriptive details you can use to develop a paragraph for each category.

(optional)

Category 1	Category 2	Category 3	Category 4

36

Step #2 Compose a Thesis and Organize Support Think about the point you want to make through your classification. In the essay about assignments, for example, the writer makes the point that better assignments lead to enjoyable learning experiences. What do you want your readers to better understand about their upcoming college experience after reading your essay?

_____

_____

_____

_____

Now compose a working thesis statement that embodies that point. Avoid statements that simply announce that you are going to classify something, such as "There are three kinds of lab partners" or "There are three ways professors lecture in college." Thesis statements of this sort lack a clear purpose.

Thesis: _____

_____

_____

Now think about how you want to present your categories. Remember, with an emphatic organization, the category you present last is what you want to most emphasize to your reader. You might want to emphasize the best of your categories as the writer of the homework essay did, or you may want to emphasize the worst of your categories, perhaps as a caution to the reader. You may even want to emphasize the middle-of-the-road category as a way to avoid either extreme. What is important is that you <u>plan</u> before writing.

Write a scratch outline for this essay. Be sure to also plan for a comparable number of details and examples to explain each category.

      Category #1

      Category #2

      Category #3

      Category #4

Step #3—Drafting   Write a first draft of this essay.

Step #4—Analyze the Draft for Revision and Revise

1. What do you do in your introduction to get your readers interested in your subject? Can you use what your readers already know about being students as a way to lead them to what they will need to know in particular as college students?
2. Look over each category you explain in your body paragraphs. For each body paragraph, do you give adequate details about what qualifies as a member of that category? Do you give examples that show the reader what you mean? Briefly list the kinds of details and examples you include in each body paragraph to make sure that you develop each in a consistent and balanced way.

Category #1
   Details that explain: _____
_____
_____

   Examples that show:_____
_____
_____

Category #2
   Details that explain: _____
_____
_____

   Examples that show:_____
_____
_____

Category #3
   Details that explain: _____
_____
_____

   Examples that show:_____
_____
_____

Category #4 (optional)
   Details that explain: _____
_____
_____

   Examples that show:_____
_____
_____

3. Check each body paragraph for coherence. Look for clear organization, transitions and repeated key words. Give a couple of examples of what you have done in the body paragraphs to make them clear for your readers to follow.

4. Look at the transitions connecting your body paragraphs. Have you avoided the easy but dull transitions? "The first category is…," "The next category is…," "The final category is …." Write out your transition sentences and look for ways to make them varied and more engaging for a reader.

First transition_____
_____

Second transition _____
_____

Third transition _____
_____

5. What final thought or insight have you given your readers in your conclusion paragraph? How have you emphasized your essay's point without simply repeating what was in the introduction?

6. Based on what you've discovered as you've answered these questions, what revisions do you plan to make to your essay?

Step #5 Edit Revised Draft

*For more practice with **classification and division**, go to www.mywritinglab.com...*
*MyWritingLab...**where better practice makes better writers!***

39

Building a Process Essay

Imagine that you have a new neighbor who has come to you for advice. He has just arrived in this country from a small village in Brazil. He speaks and reads English very well and is looking forward to attending college in the United States. What he is dreading, however, is his first trip to an American supermarket. His village has only a small farmer's market, and he has encountered nothing like the grocery stores in this country. Since you are unable to accompany him on his first trip, you agree to write an essay that explains how to go about a typical shopping trip at the local supermarket. Not only do you want to give your new friend clear and complete directions, you'd like to impress him with your writing skills.

Step #1 Brainstorming Begin by brainstorming the steps your friend should follow during his first shopping trip. He will have to purchase a lot of food and household items to stock his apartment, and, remember, he knows nothing about preparing for and shopping in a typical grocery store. Use the following prompts to help you brainstorm the various steps in this process.

Preparing for the shopping trip

Navigating the store (You may want to visit your grocery store to take note of how it is laid out.)

Finishing up and checking out

A good process also includes some warnings or some special tips at various points in the process where someone could make a mistake. Brainstorm some of these extra warnings or tips. Remember, for example, your friend knows nothing about expiration dates or comparing prices among brands.

Step #2 Compose a Thesis and Organize Support Obviously your thesis should convey that this essay is an explanation of how to shop in a U.S. grocery store, but it should probably do a bit more than that alone. Avoid such an abrupt announcement as "Here is how to shop." Instead, you may want to include some sort of positive reassurance in the thesis.

Thesis: _____

_____

_____

A process should follow a chronological organization, so you will organize the details in this essay along a timeline, beginning with the preparation for shopping and ending with loading the groceries into the car. But think carefully about how you will break these details up into paragraphs. Write a scratch outline to follow as you write your first draft. Don't forget to indicate places where you want to include special directions or warnings.

Step #3—Drafting Write a first draft of this essay. (Remember, you are writing to a very specific reader. It is appropriate to use *you* in this essay to refer to your friend.)

Step #4—Analyze the Draft for Revision and Revise

1. What do you do in the introduction to reassure your reader and to make him look forward to reading your directions?

2. What have you done to avoid paragraphs that are too long and cumbersome to read through or that are too short and choppy? What strategy did you use to arrange the process into paragraphs?

3. You don't want your directions to sound like a list. Look over your essay and make sure you have a variety of different sentence structures: simple, compound and complex. Avoid having too many very long sentences or too many short sentences back-to-back. What do you notice about the variety of sentences in your essay so far?

41

4. List some of the transitions you have used. While it's fine to use words like "Next," "Then" and "Now," you want to avoid using the same transitions over and over again.

5. Give examples of some of the warnings and special directions you have given throughout the process. Are there any more you can think of?

6. How do you end the essay? How does it reinforce—without simply repeating—the positive reassurance you give at the beginning?

7. Now put yourself in the shoes of your reader. Imagine as best you can what it would be like to step into your local grocery store for the first time. Read your essay through carefully. What steps or special concerns should you add to make this process more complete, more helpful?

8. Based on your responses to these questions, what revisions do you plan to make in this essay?

Step #5 Edit Revised Draft.

For more practice with **process**, *go to* www.mywritinglab.com... *MyWritingLab...***where better practice makes better writers!***

Analyzing a Comparison/Contrast Essay

The following draft of a classification essay has been marked up by the instructor. Revise and edit the essay according to the instructor's suggestions. Be sure to correct any other errors in the essay.

We may think that our culture's fascination with celebrities is a recent phenomenon, but the Sutherland sisters, celebrities during the late 1880s, had much in common with today's celebrities.

Like many of today's celebrities, the Sutherland Sisters began their climb to fame and fortune in the entertainment industry. The seven sisters—Sarah, Victoria, Isabella, Grace, Naomi, Dora and Mary—had lovely voices and sang at churches and local fairs around their native state of New York. Their performances always drew crowds, and by 1884 they were touring around the country with Barnum and Bailey's Greatest Show on Earth. P.T. Barnum was a famous promoter, representing the tiny Mr. and Mrs. Tom Thumb as well as the Sutherland Sisters. Also like today, audiences were not drawn simply by talent the Sutherland Sisters were strikingly attractive, and, even more important to their mass appeal, the sisters had incredibly long hair, ranging from three to seven feet in length. Long hair had been idealized as very seductive in the writing of the Victorian era. Audiences would wait spellbound for the finale of a Sutherland performance when the girls would turn their backs to reveal their floor-length tresses.

It was the publics fascination with the sisters hair that led their father to begin manufacturing and promoting a line of high-end hair products under the Sutherland name. Just as today's consumers will pay top dollar for a hair product, cosmetic or perfume endorsed by a celebrity, people flocked to buy the Sutherland Sisters products, especially their hair grower. A mixture of vegetable oil, alcohol, borax and quinine, the hair grower sold for about $1.50 per bottle at a time when salaries averaged $2 to $15 per week. Adoring fan's would mob the sisters when they showed up in local drug stores to promote there hair products, and within four years, the Sutherlands company had sold more than two million bottles of hair grower, making the Sutherlands millionaires. During this time before the Pure Food and Drug Act went into effect, anyone could put together a concoction and market it with extreme claims to its effectiveness in curing illness or growing hair.

The sisters built a lavish mansion staffed with an array of servants including special maids in charge of combing out the sisters' long hair. Each sister also had a special doll made in her likeness and with her actual hair. The seven dolls, dressed in expensive gowns, were also cared for by maids and used to promote hair products. The sisters swept through their fortune, buying clothes and jewels, traveling, and entertaining. The public followed their exploits in newspapers and magazines such as *Cosmopolitan, The New Yorker, The New*

This is a good thesis statement, but where is the rest of the introduction? Your introduction for this essay should be a short paragraph, not simply the thesis. Write a revision of the introduction.

Unity could be improved. A couple of sentences get off track of the subject and controlling idea of this paragraph. Cross them out.

Check this paragraph for a run-on.

Usage error

Apostrophes! You have five apostrophe errors in this paragraph. Find and correct them.

You have one sentence that gets off track. Cross it out.

You need a transition here. You might continue to make the connection between the sisters and contemporary celebrities.

43

York Times and *Billboard*. Stories of the Sutherland Sisters even eclipsed those of U.S. Presidents, and as one historian noted, "everything they did was news."

Unfortunately, not all the news was good. The Sutherland Sisters achieved much of the same notoriety that lands today's celebrities on the front pages of tabloids. Isabella was rumored to be the result of an illicit affair between her father and his unmarried sister-in-law. She herself created a stir when at age forty-six, she married a twenty-seven-year-old heavy-drinking playboy, who later died of a drug overdose, Isabella's second husband was sixteen years younger than she. When she was nearly fifty Victoria Sutherland also married a much younger nineteen-year-old man. Naomi Sutherland died at the young age of thirty-five and was replaced by Anne Louise Roberts whose nine feet of hair earned her a place as a "Sutherland Sister." Mary, the youngest Sutherland sister, suffered from spells of mental illness and would be locked away by the family. At the time, some people believed that long hair could deprive the brain of nourishment and cause insanity so it was in the best interest of the family to try to keep Mary's illness a secret.

By the time the last Sutherland sister died virtually penniless in 1946, the public had all but forgotten the famous sisters. Their ornate mansion, which had been bought and turned into a museum, burned to the ground in 1938 and with it much of the memorabilia of the sisters' years of fame. The Sutherland Sisters were one of the most popular entertainment acts of the 1880's, the first celebrity models and pioneers in the marketing of beauty products. But who remembers them today? Perhaps the fleeting nature of fame is what today celebrities can best learn from the Sutherland Sisters.

Margin notes:

Capitalization error

Reference error. Whom does this "she" refer to? Isabella? The sister-in-law?

Correct the comma splice.

Watch commas! You have three comma errors here.

Building a Comparison/Contrast Essay

The Hindi language film industry based in Bombay, India, known as Bollywood, rivals Hollywood as the film-making capital of the world. A comparison of the two film industries can offer a number of insights into cultural differences as well as similarities, so it is a good topic to explore in an essay.   Imagine your audience for this essay to be movie fans who know little or nothing about Bollywood.

Step #1 Brainstorming   Here are a variety of details and examples that describe the Bollywood film industry. Drawing upon what you know about U.S. movies, brainstorm a corresponding set of matching and contrasting details.

Bollywood	Hollywood
films often extravagant musicals typically three hours long with an intermission most have at least one song and dance scene woven into the script - classical Indian dance often combined with western dance elements - hero or heroine often dance with a group of supporting dancers most actors can dance few can sing, so they lip-sync songs pre-recorded by professional playback singers - playback singers featured in credits - some fans go to hear specific singers - songs can make or break movie - lyrics mostly about love films tend to be melodramatic with formulaic plots and characters - love triangles - lovers kept apart by fate/angry parents - villains - corrupt politicians some actresses won't kiss in film to avoid offending conservative fans Filmfare Awards began in 1953 - readers of *Filmfare* magazine submit votes - awards given in a lavish ceremony attended by industry stars - accused of bias towards film that are successful rather than good India government sponsors National Film Awards - President of India directs this awards ceremony - Winners determined by a government panel piracy of films a big problem - illegal DVDs appear before movie is released	

45

You can find more information about Bollywood at the following websites:

http://www.bollywoodworld.com/whatisbollywood/
http://en.wikipedia.org/wiki/Bollywood
http://mutiny.wordpress.com/2007/02/01/bollywood-vs-hollywood-the-complete-breakdown/

You can view some scenes from Bollywood movies on YouTube.

Step #2—Compose a Thesis and Organize Support Compose a thesis statement that includes what is being compared and/or contrasted and the significance of knowing these similarities and/or differences. Decide whether to use a block or a point-by-point pattern of organization.

It's not enough to simply say there are many similarities or there are many differences between Hollywood movies and Bollywood movies. If that is all the thesis does, the reader may ask, "So what?" What does a comparison of these two film industries help you to understand about people from different cultures? What do the differences reveal? What do the similarities reveal?

Before composing a thesis, brainstorm what insights one can gain from comparing these two film industries.

_____
_____
_____
_____

Working Thesis Statement: _____
_____
_____

According to your thesis statement, you are comparing _____ and
_____ with an emphasis on (similarities/differences/both) to show
that _____ .

Decide if you want to use a block organization or a point-by-point organization for this essay.

Thesis: _____	Thesis: _____

Hollywood
     1st Point_____
     2nd Point_____
     3rd Point_____
     4th Point_____
Bollywood
     1st Point_____
     2nd Point_____
     3rd Point_____
     4th Point_____
	Point #1
	     Hollywood
	     Bollywood
	Point #2
	     Hollywood
	     Bollywood
	Point #3
	     Hollywood
	     Bollywood
	Point #4
	     Hollywood
	     Bollywood

Step #3—Drafting   Write a first draft of this essay.

Step #4—Analyze the Draft for Revision and Revise

1. What have you done in your introduction to generate interest in your topic? Would any of these facts help your introduction engage your readers?

> Over 3.6 billion tickets to Bollywood films have been sold.
>
> Films from India make more money in the United States than films from any other foreign country.
>
> *Moulin Rouge*, starring Nicole Kidman and Ewan McGregor, is Australian director Baz Luhrman's tribute to Bollywood-style movies.

2. What organizational strategy does this essay follow?
    __block   __point-by-point
    How well does this organization strategy work for this subject? Are you able to avoid short, choppy paragraphs or long paragraphs that are hard to follow?

3. Have you used transitions between the paragraphs in this essay? Are the transitions predictable—"First," "Next," "Another"?   If so, can you make them more sophisticated?

    Examples: "Second, Bollywood movies differ in their subject matter." **Predictable**
    "Bollywood movies differ not only in how the actors perform, but in the plots." **More sophisticated**

4. Which examples and details in this essay do you think your readers will find most interesting?

5. Which body paragraphs need more support? What kinds of supporting details do you need to develop these paragraphs?

6. What final thought or insight does the conclusion paragraph emphasize?

7. Based on your responses to these questions, what are the main revisions you plan to make to your draft?

Step #5—Edit Revised Draft

*For more practice with **comparison/contrast**, go to www.mywritinglab.com... MyWritingLab...**where better practice makes better writers!***

47

Analyzing a Definition Essay

Read the following definition essay carefully and answer the questions that follow.

1. What does the writer do in this introduction to engage the readers?

2. Underline the thesis statement. What is this essay going to define or explain?

When my six-year-old niece Emily recently went to a friend's birthday party, she brought a present and a plastic baggie containing a small, specially-made brownie. After presents were opened and the other guests began feasting on cake, Emily ate her brownie. Emily has celiac disease, and unless a cure is found, she will never be able to join her friends in eating cake, cookies, pasta, most cereals and any of the countless other food products that contain wheat, barley or rye grains. People with celiac disease must live with a challenging diet or suffer from serious and sometimes deadly consequences.

1. Although this paragraph does not have an explicit topic sentence, it focuses on one controlling idea. What repeated key word emphasizes the focus of this paragraph?

2. Underline the sentence in this paragraph that gets off track.

3. This paragraph includes a brief definition that is crucial to the readers' understanding of celiac disease. What is defined?

Like others with celiac disease, Emily cannot eat a protein called "gluten," which is found in grains like wheat. If Emily eats any foods containing gluten, her own immune system damages the lining of her small intestine so that nutrients cannot be absorbed into her bloodstream. When Emily was a baby, before her disease was diagnosed, she was very fussy and irritable, probably because of the stomach cramps caused by the cereal in her formula. Some fussy babies suffer from colic, another type of stomach disorder. She suffered from chronic diarrhea and did not grow and put on weight like other babies her age. Unlike Emily, some people are adults or even elderly before they show symptoms of the disease, which can include chronic diarrhea or constipation, bone or joint pain, anemia, muscle cramps, and osteoporosis. While the disease may vary in the kinds of symptoms and when the symptoms begin, in all cases gluten damages the intestine, and the body becomes malnourished. The longer a person goes without treatment, the greater the risk of serious health problems including some forms of cancer.

6. This sentence serves as a transition from one main idea to the next. Which two key words in this sentence link the previous paragraph to this paragraph?

Because these various symptoms are so similar to other disorders, celiac disease is sometimes difficult to diagnose. Crohn's disease, irritable bowel syndrome, diverticulitis and chronic fatigue syndrome can all be confused with celiac disease. Emily was diagnosed early because, unfortunately, her father has the disease as well and recognized the symptoms. Celiac is a genetic disease, so it runs in families. A person who is a parent, sibling or child of someone with celiac disease has a 1 in 22 chance of having the disease as well. Although celiac disease was once thought to be uncommon in the United States, current studies estimate two million people with the disease. With the growing awareness of this disease, doctors and health care providers are more likely to diagnose it when symptoms first appear.

7. Give two examples of specific facts the writer incorporates into this paragraph.

Once diagnosed with celiac disease, people must face the challenge of a gluten-free diet for the rest of their lives. This means they cannot eat foods and products containing wheat, barley and rye, no matter how small the amount. Besides avoiding the obvious products like pastas and cereals, people with celiac disease must carefully read labels. Many processed foods contain gluten additives, and unless a processed food product is labeled "gluten free," it should be avoided. Even some medicines contain gluten. There are, however, plenty of foods people with celiac disease can enjoy, like fresh fruits and vegetables, meat and fish and rice. In addition, many grocery stores carry gluten-free products. Emily's mother was able to find Emily's favorite brownies, which are made with rice flour, in the gluten-free section of the local grocery store. Once on a gluten-free diet, Emily and most other celiac patients recover completely from any damage to their small intestines and live healthy lives.

8. According to this sentence, what will this body paragraph focus on?

9. Give two examples of specific examples the writer uses in this paragraph to add interest and clarity.

Knowing Emily and the adjustments she has had to make in her life to accommodate her disease has made me more sensitive to those with special needs, especially those involving diet. When my own grocery store recently opened a gluten-free section, I sent a note of thanks to the manager. And someday, when I am having birthday parties for my own children, I will be sure to find out if any of the young partygoers have food allergies or special dietary needs like Emily.

10. How does the writer connect the conclusion to the introduction?

11. What do you think is the most significant final thought the writer tries to leave with the readers?

12. How do the references to Emily and her family help the readers better under celiac disease?

13. Which of the following do you think would make the best title for this essay? Briefly explain why.

        a. Defining Celiac Disease
        b. No Cake for Emily
        c. Diet Disaster
        d. Understanding Celiac Disease
        e. Hurray for Gluten-Free Products

14. What additional information about celiac disease do you think the writer should have included? Could this information be incorporated into any of the existing paragraphs, or would it need a new paragraph? If it needs a new paragraph, where in the essay should that paragraph be?

Building a Definition Essay

Write an essay in which you define a "condition" that you or someone you know has. Your goal is to help those who may not know the implications of this condition understand them better. Use the experiences of a real person who has this condition to make the information in your definition more "real," more engaging for your readers.

Step #1 Brainstorming and Freewriting   First, brainstorm ten or so conditions you might write about. The condition could be a medical condition or it might describe a person whose life is profoundly impacted by a particular personality trait or interest such as a social butterfly or a baseball fanatic. For each condition, be sure that you know of a real person whom you can use as an example to illustrate the condition just as the writer of the definition essay used Emily's experiences to help define celiac disease.

_____   _____
_____   _____
_____   _____
_____   _____
_____   _____

Choose the most promising topic from your list and do some focused freewriting to generate some facts and examples you can use in your definition.

_____
_____
_____
_____
_____
_____
_____
_____
_____
_____

Step #2   Compose a Thesis and Organize Support   Think about the point you want your definition to make. Your thesis needs to let the reader know the subject being defined and the point you want to make with that definition. For example, in the essay about celiac disease, the thesis emphasizes the challenging nature of accommodating the disease.

Brainstorm some points about the condition you are defining that you want your paper to emphasize:

_____
_____
_____
_____
_____

51

Working Thesis Statement: _____

_____

_____

_____

According to this thesis, your essay will define the condition of _____

and the point about that condition the essay will emphasize is _____

_____

_____

Now think about a logical way to organize your support for this thesis. In the essay about celiac disease the author used this organization:

I.   Symptoms

II.   Difficulty of Diagnoses

III.   Treatment through Diet

Write a scratch outline to follow for your first draft.

Step #3—Drafting   Write a first draft of this essay.

Step #4—Analyze the Draft for Revision and Revise

1. What in your introduction catches the readers' interest? In the essay on celiac disease, the writer begins with a short scenario that shows how the disease impacts a particular person. Would that introductory device improve your introduction?

2. What organization strategy did you use to organize the paragraphs in this essay? Does it allow you to clearly connect the paragraphs?

3. What kinds of transitional devices do you use to connect the paragraphs in this essay?
   a. Single word transitions like *next, also*
   b. Transitional phrases that lead from the previous topic to the new topic
   c. A combination of single word transitions and transitional phrases

   What might you do to improve the transitions?

4. Does each paragraph have a clear controlling idea that supports the thesis? Briefly explain the connection between each paragraph and the thesis.

   Thesis: _____

   _____

         CI #1_____
         CI #2_____
         CI #3_____
         CI #4_____

5. What are some of the key words you repeat in this essay?

6. Besides the condition that the essay defines, are there other words or terms that needed defining in this essay? What are they?

7. Give two examples of specific details you use in this essay.

8. Give two examples of vivid examples you use to add clarity and interest.

9. Briefly describe how you conclude the essay. Did you choose to refer back to the introduction in any way? What final thought do you leave with the reader?

10. Based on your answers to these questions, what revisions do you plan to make to this essay?

Step #5 Edit Revised Draft

*For more practice with **definition**, go to www.mywritinglab.com... MyWritingLab...**where better practice makes better writers!***

Building a Persuasion Letter

Imagine that you are a business major at a prestigious university. For two years you have taken general education courses, and now, beginning your junior year, you will be taking upper level business courses through the university's College of Business.

Recently, controversy has erupted over the College of Business's mandatory dress code. Students taking courses through the College of Business must wear casual business attire when attending classes and formal business attire when engaged in internships or other interactions with the outside business community. This means when you take your business classes, you will no longer be able to wear flip-flops, sandals, athletic shoes, jeans, cargo pants or t-shirts to class. In fact, professors are allowed to expel from their classes any students who do not adhere to the college's dress code. College administrators say the dress code is part of the college's "total program" in preparing students for the business world and cite the college's strong record in placing its students in high-paying jobs after graduation. A growing number of students within the college, however, claim the dress code is restrictive and unnecessary. They say students have the right to wear comfortable and more affordable clothes to their regular classes and can be expected to dress appropriately when working in the business community without a mandated dress code.

As the higher level university administration attempts to resolve this issue, it has asked for letters from students like yourself, giving your opinion on what should be done. Write a letter to the university president, Dr. Wright, that states your position on this mandatory dress code and the reasons you've taken that stand.

Step #1 Brainstorming As you prepare your argument, try to get a strong overview of both sides by brainstorming reasons and examples that support both sides of the argument.

Keep the Dress Code As It Is	Abolish or Change the Dress Code

Once you have established which side of the argument you will support, you will need to decide how you will counter or refute your opponent's arguments. List what you think might be your opponent's strongest reasons or examples and then brainstorm the counterarguments you will use to refute them.

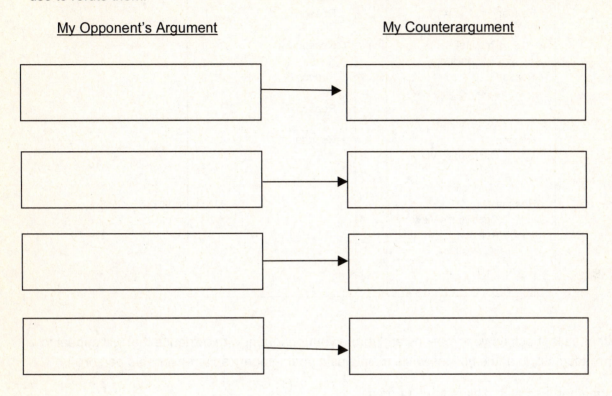

My Opponent's Argument   My Counterargument

Step #2 Compose a Thesis and Organize Support

Your thesis needs to clearly state what your position is on this controversy. State your position respectfully yet emphatically. Do not clutter your thesis with unnecessary fillers like "I think" or "I feel" since they make you sound wavering and unsure of yourself.

Thesis: _____

_____

_____

In putting together your outline, you should consider organizing your reasons for your position emphatically—that is from your least to your most convincing reason. Also, consider where you will place your rebuttal of the opposing view. You can deal with the rebuttal throughout the essay or in one section.

Examples:

Thesis	Thesis
Reason 1	Reason 1
Opponent's View	
Rebuttal	Reason 2
My Position	
Reason 2	Reason 3
Opponent's View	
Rebuttal	Reason 4
My Position	
Reason 3	Rebuttal
Opponent's View	
Rebuttal	
My Position	
Reason 4	
Opponent's View	
Rebuttal	
My Position	

In either case, back up your reasons and refute your opponent with evidence that will appeal to your readers' logic and emotions while maintaining your integrity as a reasonable person.

Put together a scratch outline for your draft.

Step #3—Drafting   Write a first draft of this essay.

Step #4—Analyze the Draft for Revision and Revise

1. Since you are writing a letter, you will, of course, begin with a salutation—i.e. Dear Dr. Wright. Since this is a formal letter, be sure to put a colon after the salutation instead of a comma, which is used in informal letters.

2. In the first paragraph of your letter, you probably want to establish who you are and what your position on this issue is. It is also important that you set a positive tone. You want to present yourself as a student who wants only what will be best for both the students and the institution. Briefly explain how you have done this.

How have you introduced yourself and established your interest in this controversy?

Where does your thesis appear in this first paragraph and how is it stated?

What have you done to set a positive tone?

3. Look at how you have presented the reasons for taking your position. What did you decide is the most important reason and why? Did you place this reason in an emphatic position near the end of the letter?

4. What kinds of evidence did you use to back up your reasons? Give at least three examples of what you think is your best supporting evidence.

5. How did you handle the rebuttal of your opponent's arguments? Did you address them all at once or throughout the letter? Why did you decide upon this strategy?

6. Since this is a letter to the university president, you want to maintain a respectful tone and a somewhat formal style. Give examples of two of your sentences that do this.

7. What is the strategy you used in the concluding paragraph of your letter? What final thought do you leave with the president?

8. Based on your responses to the questions, what do you plan to revise in this letter?

Step #5 Edit Revised Draft

*For more practice with **persuasion and argument**, go to www.mywritinglab.com... MyWritingLab...**where better practice makes better writers!***

ANSWER KEY

Audience Awareness Key

As part of their application process, job applicants were asked to write about their skills and abilities. Their audience is the employer who will determine whether or not to give them a job.

First, think about the audience. What do you think a prospective employer will want to see in this piece of writing in terms of content, tone and style?

Employers want to know what talents and abilities applicants can bring to the company to make it more efficient, more profitable. They want someone who will do more than merely what is expected. The writer should give specific examples that showcase workplace skills. The tone should be confident, and the style should be formal but not pretentious. There should be no obvious sentence errors.

Now read the following excerpts from the job applications and evaluate how well the applicants addressed their audience and achieved their purpose of standing out as the best candidate for the job.

1. I have learned to multi-task at my current job at a video rental store. I can straighten shelves, wait on customers, take phone orders, and update inventory orders and still have time to work on my homework for my college classes.

What does this writer do well to reach the audience and achieve her purpose?

This writer does a good job of illustrating her abilities. Multi-tasking is a skill many employers would appreciate in their employees.

What could the writer do to better impress her audience and achieve her purpose?

It's not a good idea to tell an employer that she does homework while on the job. Most employers want employees to concentrate on what they are being paid for and not outside work.

2. I communicate well with other people. I am doing very well in my english and communications classes. I was also one of ten students picked to be conflict mediators for other students who where having conflicts with there peers or sometimes even there teachers.

59

What does this writer do well to reach the audience and achieve his purpose?

Communication skills are important to most employers, so this is a good trait to emphasize. And when someone does not yet have a lot of experience in the workplace, drawing on examples from school can be an effective alternative.

What could the writer do to better impress the audience and achieve his purpose?

The writer needs to do a much better job of proofreading. Obvious errors, like not capitalizing *English* and confusing *where* and *were* and *there* and *their* will not impress an employer.

3. At my last job in a retail department store, I started as a sales assistant and earned five customer services awards. Then I was promoted to a customer service specialist. Working for your company would allow me to continue to increase my earning potential.

What does this writer do well to reach the audience and achieve his purpose?

By mentioning awards and promotions, this writer does a good job of *showing* his ability to work well with customers.

What could the writer do to better impress the audience and achieve his purpose?

Employers are more interested in how an applicant can help the company, not how the company can help an applicant. The writer would do better to emphasize how his skills can be put to work at the employer's business.

4. I am a dependable person cause I show up to work and on time every day. Sometimes I stay late just so I can finish my work.

What does this writer do well to reach the audience and achieve her purpose?

Dependability is a trait most employers look for in their applicants. Also, employers appreciated an employee's being willing to work late when necessary.

What could the writer do to better impress her audience and achieve her purpose?

Employers expect all employees to show up and to be on time. A serious job applicant needs to show how she will go beyond what is merely expected. Also, an employer might wonder whether or not she's staying late because she can't get her work done

efficiently during the regular working hours. Finally, *cause* is not an appropriate substitute for *because*.

The Thesis Statement Key

Just as a topic sentence presents the subject and controlling idea of a paragraph, the thesis presents the subject and controlling idea of an essay. Like a topic sentence, the thesis should present the writer's point. It should take a stand or present an opinion about the subject.

Identify each of the following as an announcement (A), too broad (B), too narrow (N) or a thesis statement (T).

B   There are many problems with computers.

A   This essay will discuss the dangers of computer viruses.

T   You can take some simple precautions to protect your computer from viruses.

N   If your computer makes unusual sounds or randomly plays music, it may have a virus.

T   As gas prices continue to rise, the unique Aptera may soon be the vehicle of choice for many Americans.

N   The Aptera prototype gets 230 miles per gallon of gas, but the manufacturer is aiming for over 300 miles per gallon.

A   I want to convince you to buy an Aptera.

B   The high price of gasoline has greatly impacted the United States.

N   In 1868 Thomas Henry Huxley first suggested birds and reptiles had a common ancestor.

T   Strong evidence supports the theory that birds evolved from dinosaurs.

B   Fossils can teach us many things about the past.

A   In this paper I will show how birds may have evolved from dinosaurs.

T   The Cardiff Giant hoax of 1869 captured headlines with its controversies.

B   People have enjoyed hoaxes for centuries.

A   Let's look at how hoaxes trick people.

N   The famous showman P.T. Barnum joined in the Cardiff Giant Hoax.

N   *Godzilla* is one of the most famous monster films of the 1950's.

A   My essay will compare the American version of *Godzilla* with the Japanese version.

T   For the Japanese, the original *Godzilla* was a high quality film with a powerful message.

B   Movies say a lot about the time and culture in which they are made.

B   Environment plays an important role in our lives.

T   Some simple changes in your workplace environment can greatly reduce stress.

N   Poor lighting can cause workplace stress.

A   Here are the ways you can reduce stress in the workplace.

Essay Unity Key

The topic sentence of each body paragraph in an essay must support the thesis statement. In each of the following sets, circle the letter of the topic sentence that does not support the thesis statement.

1. Thesis: Participation in extracurricular clubs and activities is an important part of the college experience.
    e. Some organizations will allow you to practice skills needed for your target career.
    (f.) Getting overextended through too many commitments to organizations can cause your grades to suffer.
    g. Joining organizations can be a way to meet others who share your interests.
    h. Holding office in an organization will show future employers that you have leadership skills.

2. Thesis: New managers often make some basic mistakes in their leadership roles.
    e. New managers may confuse discipline with punishment in dealing with employees.
    f. New managers may feel dependent upon employees and tolerate inadequate work performance.
    g. New managers may feel sorry for employees and become too understanding of poor performance.
    (h.) New managers can benefit from a mentor program that matches them with a higher level administrator.

3. Thesis: Because living together is not the same as "hanging out," best friends need to take steps to assure a successful relationship as roommates.
    e. Best friends need to accept that people change and learn to adapt.
    f. Friends should establish some ground rules before moving in together.
    (g.) Sharing an apartment is more stressful and demanding than sharing a dorm room.
    h. Best friends should be prepared for stress and how to handle it constructively.

4. Thesis: Successful employees know how to balance their personal and professional lives.
    (e.) College internships can provide you important on-the-job training that classroom work cannot duplicate.
    f. Sharing too many personal details of your life at work can negatively affect your professional reputation.
    g. Not sharing anything about your personal life may keep your fellow employees from feeling connected to you.

h. There are some basic guidelines to follow when discussing your personal life at the office.

Organizing Details into a Unified Paragraphs Key

Thesis Statement: The reasons behind the nicknames of our states are as diverse as the states themselves.

I. Some nicknames recall significant events within a state's history.

A. Delaware laid claim to the nickname "First State" since in 1787, it was the first state to ratify the U.S. Constitution.

B. While not the first to sign the U.S. Constitution, Connecticut took the nickname the "Constitution State" because some historians claim that the first constitution in history was written there.

C. Another state that chose its nickname based upon having a "first" is Wyoming, known as the "Equality State" for being the first to give women the right to vote, to hold public office and to serve on juries.

D. California took the nickname the "Golden State" because its development was spurred by the discovery of gold in 1848.

E. Because the volunteer soldiers from Tennessee served with distinction under General Andrew Jackson at the Battle of New Orleans during the War of 1812, Tennessee is known as the "Volunteer State."

II. Distinctive geographical features are another source of nicknames.

A. Arizona, of course, calls itself the "Grand Canyon State."

B. Illinois, the "Prairie State" takes pride in celebrating and preserving its sweeping prairies.

C. With borders touching four of the five Great Lakes, Michigan calls itself the "Great Lakes State."

D. Perhaps because it couldn't choose just one of its geographical features or part of its natural beauty to celebrate, Arkansas is known as the "Natural State."

III. Some states base their nicknames on what grows well in the native soil.

A. The bluish-purple buds of its native grass gave Kentucky the nickname the "Bluegrass State."

B. The "Buckeye State," Ohio took its nickname from the many buckeye trees that once thrived there.

C. Great forests of native evergreens gave nicknames to two states: Maine, the "Pine Tree State" and Washington, the "Evergreen State."

D. Kansas took its nickname the "Sunflower State," from the wild flowers that dotted its expansive plains.

Missouri proudly calls itself the "Show-Me State," a nickname that acknowledges common sense as well as stubbornness.

Iowa is known as the "Hawkeye State" in honor of Chief Black Hawk.

Oregon took the name the "Beaver State" in honor of one of its native animals, which had been hunted to near extinction before protective measures re-established its presence in the state's rivers and streams.

Analyzing a Narrative Essay Key

Carefully read the following narrative essay and answer the questions that follow.

Floyd Collins, the son of a poor farmer, grew up exploring caves in the region of Kentucky long famous for its fabulous caverns. Crystal Cave, located on the Collins' farm, had exceptionally beautiful crystal formations, but attracted few tourists because the cave was so far from the main road leading to popular and profitable Mammoth Cave. Hoping to find another entrance to Mammoth Cave or a new cave closer to the tourists' route, Floyd began exploring other caves in the region and soon found what he thought was a promising venture in Sand Cave. On Friday, January 30, 1925, Floyd was crawling out through a narrow passage in Sand Cave when he dislodged a rock from the ceiling, pinning his leg and trapping him.

When family and friends found Floyd the next morning, they tried everything they could to get him out, but Floyd was stuck tight. By Monday morning, newspapers around the country had picked up the story, and soon the relatively new media of radio was broadcasting regular updates of the rescue efforts. Firefighters, geologists, stone masons and mining experts arrived with advice on how to rescue Floyd. A college president offered to send in his basketball team to dig Floyd out, and an heiress from Chicago offered to send her surgeon to amputate Floyd's leg. Eventually, there were over three hundred volunteer rescuers, fifty reporters from newspapers all over the country, and nearly twenty thousand spectators on hand for the Sand Cave rescue. Even vendors appeared, selling food, drinks and souvenirs to the crowds.

While the would-be rescuers were able to reach Floyd to give him some milk and juice, they made no progress towards freeing him from the tunnel. At one point, Skeets Miller, a young reporter from a Louisville newspaper, squeezed down the tunnel and interviewed the weakening Floyd. While the interview did little to help Floyd, Miller later won the Pulitzer Prize for his daring reporting of the story. Shortly after Miller's interviews, the tunnel above Floyd collapsed, completely cutting him off from the outside. Rescuers began digging a shaft to try to reach Floyd, and finally on February 16, they found the unlucky cave explorer dead from starvation and exposure.

Today, the historical marker outside Sand Cave says that Floyd's story "Aroused the sympathy of a nation." Was it sympathy that made Floyd's story one of the biggest news events of the time, or simply morbid curiosity fueled by an aggressive news media? Whatever caused it, the fascination with Floyd's ordeal continued long after his death, inspiring books, a movie, a documentary and even a musical. Floyd went into Sand Cave a poor Kentucky backwoodsman and emerged a folk hero.

1. The introduction of a narrative essay often answers the same questions as the opening paragraph of a good newspaper story: Who? What? When? Where? Why? Look over the introduction paragraph and see if it gives you the answers to the following questions.

Who is this story about? **Floyd Collins**

When does this story take place? **January 30 to February16, 1925**

Where does this story take place? **Kentucky cave region**

What happens in this story? **Floyd becomes trapped in a cave and a media circus erupts around the attempts to rescue him.**

Why did this happen?   **Floyd took a foolish risk because he wanted so much to be able to make money by attracting tourists to a cave on his family's land. The media may have exploited the public's morbid curiosity about such a horrifying predicament.**

2. What in this introduction makes readers curious and want to read on?

    Answers will vary.

3. What do the details in the first body paragraph suggest to you about the rescue attempt? How well planned was it? What seems to be the priority of the people gathered outside Sand Cave?

    Rescue attempts seemed poorly planned—haphazard and chaotic. People seemed gathered more out of curiosity than any real desire to go into the cave a rescue Floyd.

4. What kind of organization pattern does this essay follow? Give examples of some of the transitions the writer uses throughout the essay.

    Chronological

    "When family and friends found Floyd the next morning…"
    "By Monday morning…"
    "Eventually…"
    "Shortly after Miller's interviews…"
    "today…"
    --and others

5. The Sand Cave rescue was one of the biggest news stories of its time. Why do you think so many people were fascinated by this drama as it played out? Why do you think this story continued to fascinate people for decades after it happened?

   Answers will vary.

6. The writer of this narrative does not explicitly state the point of the story, and there are several possible. What do you think is the main point of this essay? What are some other possible lessons? **Answers will vary.**

7. Sometimes the writer of a short narrative must make hard decisions about what details to include or not include. The following are additional details about Floyd Collins' story that the writer might have included. Put the letter of the detail where you think it would best fit in the essay. Cross out details you would not include.

   Answers may vary somewhat.

a. Floyd's body was left in the tunnel, and the family held a funeral service at the surface.

b. Floyd's own father worked the crowds during the rescue, posing for photographs and handing out flyers promoting Crystal Cave.

c. ~~It cost $1 to enter Mammoth Cave and $4 to stay all day.~~

d. ~~Skeet Miller fed Floyd milk through a rubber hose and tried unsuccessfully to lift the rock off with a jack.~~

e. In April Floyd's family retrieved his body from the cave and buried him near crystal cave.

f. Doctors estimated that Floyd died sometime between February 12 and February 16.

g. Floyd was trapped 125 feet below ground in a space 8 inches high and 12 feet long.

h. ~~Floyd discovered Crystal Cave on his father's farm when he chased a ground hog down a hole.~~

i. After Floyd's family sold Crystal Cave, the new owners moved Floyd's body to a glass-topped coffin and exhibited it in Crystal Cave until vandals stole the body in 1929.

j. ~~The Louisville newspaper described Skeet Miller as a hero.~~

k. The boulder that wedged against Floyd's leg weighed less than 27 pounds.

l. At one point, rescuers tried to pull Floyd out with a harness.

m. When Floyd's stolen body was found, with its left leg missing and never recovered, it was returned to the glass-topped coffin, which was chained and kept in a secluded part of Crystal Cave.

n. The Kentucky governor sent in two detachments of soldiers to maintain order, and the Red Cross set up a field hospital outside Sand Cave.

o. When Floyd's family could not free him, they offered a $500 reward for his rescue.

p. In 1961, the Mammoth Cave National Park System bought and closed Crystal Cave, and at his family's request, Floyd's body was finally buried in a local cemetery in 1989.

q. ~~Floyd went into the cave alone without proper clothing or equipment, which was very foolish.~~

Introduction paragraph

First body paragraph

b
g
k
l
n
o

Second body paragraph

f

A new third body paragraph

a
e
i
m
p

Conclusion paragraph

Analyzing a Classification Essay Key

The following draft of a classification essay has been marked up by the instructor. Revise and edit the essay according to the instructor's suggestions.

Homework Hierarchy

> The essay needs a more engaging title. **Answers will vary.**

Throughout their academic careers, students will have to deal with homework. For those who pursue higher education, the homework bar is set at new heights. Seldom are there classes that don't require hours of outside homework that cut into time that could be spent earning money to pay for more classes or just relaxing with friends and family. However, not all homework is created equal. Homework assignments can range from mind-numbing wastes of time to truly engaging learning experiences.

> Can you find a way to avoid this cliché?

Students are most frustrated by the homework they think is a waste of their time. These assignments do not clearly connect to the goals of the class, nor do they engage the students' interest. For example, I once had a composition teacher who assigned a list of 100 trivia questions for the class to answer by using only print sources in the library. After more than eight hours of library work, I knew such facts as when the Mongols first invaded China and the depth of Crater Lake in California. An hour tour of the library before a research paper assignment would have been more practical and helpful because what was learned could be immediately applied to an assignment. In another class, a psychology teacher required each student to read ten outside articles that dealt with any kind of "social interaction" and write up a one page summary of each article. Each summary earned a checkmark at the top and ten points but, while easy to complete, did little to help anyone better understand what was covered in the rest of the course. Rather than helping students learn, these kinds of assignments are more like little hurdles for them to overcome in order to pass a class.

> Check punctuation. You have two errors in this sentence.

> Can you briefly tell why this assignment would have been better?

> A transition would make this next example seem less abrupt.

> You unnecessarily shift person here.

A little less frustrating are those assignments that meet the goals of the class but do not excite or interest the students. Long reading assignments in history, for instance, are often boring to get through, but if the material helps students better understand **the subject** and do well on tests, the assignment is tolerable. Working through twenty algebra equations may be the kind of practice that leads to a perfect score on a test, but for some students, ten practice equations would do the trick. ~~I'm not even a math major, and I can understand how to do an equation after solving four or five.~~ **Similarly,** composition teachers often assign topics for papers that hold no interest whatsoever for students. These assignments probably teach something about writing, but they are such a chore to write that students sometimes do poorly because they are bored or frustrated by them. Students can better tolerate these kinds of assignments that may help them understand the course material because certain required classes have to be passed whether they interest students or not. ~~I, for example, have three more general education classes to complete, and then I can focus on classes in my major, which is horticulture.~~

Thankfully, there are those homework assignments that catch students up in the excitement of learning. For example, I once had a business teacher who gave us case studies involving typical problems encounters in the business world that students had to solve. Not only did completing these case studies help me better understand the business concepts covered on the exam, but the interesting and real world problems gave helpful insights into what I might encountered in a business career. These case studies were practical and even fun to work on, and I found that homework to be some of the best of my college career. Assignments that are kind of different and teach useful information make students want to learn.

It's likely homework will always take up a good chunk of **college students' lives.** Also, it's not likely that every assignment will please **them.** However, teachers can make homework a more rewarding experience for most students by making sure it relates to the class and when possible, adding a little extra fun and excitement to the homework mix.

Analyzing a Comparison/Contrast Essay Key

The following draft of a classification essay has been marked up by the instructor. Revise and edit the essay according to the instructor's suggestions.

We may think that our culture's fascination with celebrities is a recent phenomenon, but the Sutherland sisters, celebrities during the late 1880s, had much in common with today's celebrities.

Like many of today's celebrities, the Sutherland Sisters began their climb to fame and fortune in the entertainment industry. The seven sisters—Sarah, Victoria, Isabella, Grace, Naomi, Dora and Mary—had lovely voices and sang at churches and local fairs around their native state of New York. Their performances always drew crowds, and by 1884 they were touring around the country with Barnum and Bailey's Greatest Show on Earth. ~~P.T. Barnum was a famous promoter, representing the tiny Mr. and Mrs. Tom Thumb as well as the Sutherland Sisters.~~ Also like today, audiences were not drawn simply by **talent. The** Sutherland Sisters were strikingly attractive, and, even more important to their mass appeal, the sisters had incredibly long hair, ranging from three to seven feet in length. ~~Long hair had been idealized as very seductive in the writing of the Victorian era.~~ Audiences would wait spellbound for the finale of a Sutherland performance when the girls would turn their backs to reveal their floor-length tresses.

It was the **public's** fascination with the **sisters'** hair that led their father to begin manufacturing and promoting a line of high-end hair products under the Sutherland name. Just as today's consumers will pay top dollar for a hair product, cosmetic or perfume endorsed by a celebrity, people flocked to buy the Sutherland **Sisters'** products, especially their hair grower. A mixture of vegetable oil, alcohol, borax and quinine, the hair grower sold for about $1.50 per bottle at a time when salaries averaged $2 to $15 per week. Adoring **fans** would mob the sisters when they showed up in local drug stores to promote **their** hair products, and within four years, the **Sutherlands'** company had sold more than two million bottles of hair grower, making the Sutherlands millionaires. ~~During this time before the Pure Food and Drug Act went into effect, anyone could put together a concoction and market it with extreme claims to its effectiveness in curing illness or growing hair.~~

With their new-found wealth, the Sutherland Sisters soon had a lifestyle to rival any of today's top movie stars. The sisters built a lavish mansion staffed with an array of servants including special maids in charge of combing out the sisters' long hair. Each sister also had a special doll made in her likeness and with her actual hair. The seven dolls, dressed in expensive gowns, were also cared for by maids and used to promote hair products. The

This is a good thesis statement, but where is the rest of the introduction? Your introduction for this essay should be a short paragraph, not simply the thesis. Write a revision of the introduction. **Revisions will vary.**

Unity could be improved. A couple of sentences get off track of the subject and controlling idea of this paragraph. Cross them out. **See crossed out sentences.**

Check this paragraph for a run-on.

Apostrophes! You have five apostrophe errors in this paragraph. Find and correct them.

Usage error

You have one sentence that gets off track. Cross it out.

You need a transition here. You might continue to make the connection between the sisters and contemporary celebrities.

Capitalization error

Reference error. Whom does this "she" refer to? Isabella? The sister-in-law?

Correct the comma splice.

Watch commas! You have three comma errors here.

sisters swept through their fortune, buying clothes and jewels, traveling, and entertaining. The public followed their exploits in newspapers and magazines such as *Cosmopolitan, The New Yorker, The New York Times* and *Billboard.* Stories of the Sutherland Sisters even eclipsed those of U.S. Presidents, and as one historian noted, "Everything they did was news."

Unfortunately, not all the news was good. The Sutherland Sisters achieved much of the same notoriety that lands today's celebrities on the front pages of tabloids. Isabella was rumored to be the result of an illicit affair between her father and his unmarried sister-in-law. Isabella herself created a stir when at age forty-six, she married a twenty-seven-year-old heavy-drinking playboy, who later died of a drug overdose. Isabella's second husband was sixteen years younger than she. When she was nearly fifty, Victoria Sutherland also married a much younger nineteen-year-old man. Naomi Sutherland died at the young age of thirty-five and was replaced by Anne Louise Roberts, whose nine feet of hair earned her a place as a "Sutherland Sister." Mary, the youngest away by the family. At the time, some people believed that long hair could deprive the brain of nourishment and cause insanity, so it was in the best interest of the family to try to keep Mary's illness a secret.

By the time the last Sutherland sister died virtually penniless in 1946, the public had all but forgotten the famous sisters. Their ornate mansion, which had been bought and turned into a museum, burned to the ground in 1938 and with it much of the memorabilia of the sisters' years of fame. The Sutherland Sisters were one of the most popular entertainment acts of the 1880's, the first celebrity models and pioneers in the marketing of beauty products. But who remembers them today? Perhaps the fleeting nature of fame is what today celebrities can best learn from the Sutherland Sisters.

Analyzing a Definition Essay Key

Read the following definition essay carefully and answer the questions that follow.

When my six-year-old niece Emily recently went to a friend's birthday party, she brought a present and a plastic baggie containing a small, specially-made brownie. After presents were opened and the other guests began feasting on cake, Emily ate her brownie. Emily has celiac disease, and unless a cure is found, she will never be able to join her friends in eating cake, cookies, pasta, most cereals and any of the countless other food products that contain wheat, barley or rye grains. **People with celiac disease must live with a challenging diet or suffer from serious and sometimes deadly consequences.**

Like others with celiac disease, Emily cannot eat a protein called "gluten," which is found in grains like wheat. If Emily eats any foods containing gluten, her own immune system damages the lining of her small intestine so that nutrients cannot be absorbed into her bloodstream. When Emily was a baby, before her disease was diagnosed, she was very fussy and irritable, probably because of the stomach cramps caused by the cereal in her formula. **Some fussy babies suffer from colic, another type of stomach disorder.** She suffered from chronic diarrhea and did not grow and put on weight like other babies her age. Unlike Emily, some people are adults or even elderly before they show symptoms of the disease, which can include chronic diarrhea or constipation, bone or joint pain, anemia, muscle cramps, and osteoporosis. While the disease may vary in the kinds of symptoms and when the symptoms begin, in all cases gluten damages the intestine, and the body becomes malnourished. The longer a person goes without treatment, the greater the risk of serious health problems including some forms of cancer.

Because these various symptoms are so similar to other disorders, celiac disease is sometimes difficult to diagnose. Crohn's disease, irritable bowel syndrome, diverticulitis and chronic fatigue syndrome can all be confused with celiac disease. Emily was diagnosed early because, unfortunately, her father has the disease as well and recognized the symptoms. Celiac is a genetic disease, so it runs in families. A person who is a parent, sibling or child of

---

1. What does the writer do in this introduction to engage the readers? **The writer puts a "face" on the disease by connecting it to an actual person in a situation most of the readers can relate to.**

2. Underline the thesis statement. What is this essay going to define or explain? **The essay will define celiac disease.**

3. Although this paragraph does not have an explicit topic sentence, it focuses on one controlling idea. What repeated key word emphasizes the focus of this paragraph? **symptoms**

4. Underline the sentence in this paragraph that gets off track.

5. This paragraph includes a brief definition that is crucial to the readers' understanding of celiac disease. What is defined? **gluten**

6. This sentence serves as a transition from one main idea to the next. Which two key words in this sentence link the previous paragraph to this paragraph? **symptoms** and **diagnose**

7. Give two examples of specific facts the writer incorporates into this paragraph.
A person with close family members who have the disease has a 1 in 22 chance of having it. Two million people in the United States have celiac disease.

8. According to this sentence, what will this body paragraph focus on?
The challenge of a gluten-free diet

9. Give two examples of specific examples the writer uses in this paragraph to add interest and clarity.
Answers will vary.

10. How does the writer connect the conclusion to the introduction?
The writer refers back to the birthday party in the first paragraph.

11. What do you think is the most significant final thought the writer tries to leave with the readers?
Answers will vary.

someone with celiac disease has a 1 in 22 chance of having the disease as well. Although celiac disease was once thought to be uncommon in the United States, current studies estimate two million people with the disease. With the growing awareness of this disease, doctors and health care providers are more likely to diagnose it when symptoms first appear.

Once diagnosed with celiac disease, people must face the challenge of a gluten-free diet for the rest of their lives. This means they cannot eat foods and products containing wheat, barley and rye, no matter how small the amount. Besides avoiding the obvious products like pastas and cereals, people with celiac disease must carefully read labels. Many processed foods contain gluten additives, and unless a processed food product is labeled "gluten free," it should be avoided. Even some medicines contain gluten. There are, however, plenty of foods people with celiac disease can enjoy, like fresh fruits and vegetables, meat and fish and rice. In addition, many grocery stores carry gluten-free products. Emily's mother was able to find Emily's favorite brownies, which are made with rice flour, in the gluten-free section of the local grocery store. Once on a gluten-free diet, Emily and most other celiac patients recover completely from any damage to their small intestines and live healthy lives.

Knowing Emily and the adjustments she has had to make in her life to accommodate her disease has made me more sensitive to those with special needs, especially those involving diet. When my own grocery store recently opened a gluten-free section, I sent a note of thanks to the manager. And someday when I am having birthday parties for my own children, I will be sure to find out if any of the young partygoers have food allergies or special dietary needs like Emily.

12. How do the references to Emily and her family help the readers better under celiac disease?

Answers will vary.

73

13. Which of the following do you think would make the best title for this essay? Briefly explain why.

      a. Defining Celiac Disease
      b. No Cake for Emily
      c. Diet Disaster
      d. Understanding Celiac Disease
      e. Hurray for Gluten-Free Products

Answers will vary.

14. What additional information about celiac disease do you think the writer should have included? Could this information be incorporated into any of the existing paragraphs, or would it need a new paragraph? If it needs a new paragraph, where in the essay should that paragraph be?

Answers will vary.

Essay Workbook Resources

Audience and Purpose—no sources

Audience Awareness—no sources

The Thesis Statement

>http://auto.howstuffworks.com/aptera-hybrid.htm/printable
>www.aptera.com/
>http://www.abc.net.au/science/slab/dinobird/story.htm
>http://www.enchantedlearning.com/subjects/dinosaurs/Dinobirds.html
>http://www.trivia-library.com/b/famous-hoaxes-history-of-the-cardiff-giant.htm

>http://www.dukenews.duke.edu/2004/06/godzilla_0604._print.ht
>http://www.psychwww.com/mtsite/smimpenv.html

Essay Unity

>http://www.campusblues.com/best-friends-roommates.asp
>http://www.workrelationships.com/site/articles/performance_management.htm

Organizing Details into Paragraphs

>http://50states.com/

Developing an Essay with Supporting Details I—no sources

Developing an Essay with Supporting Details II—no sources

Expanding a Cause and Effect Paragraph into an Essay

>http://www.forbes.com/business/2006/05/03/business-basics-stupid-firing-cx_sr_0504sacked.html
>http://hubpages.com/hub/Fired

Building a Description Essay—no sources

Analyzing a Narrative Essay

>http://en.wikipedia.org/wiki/Floyd_Collins_(person)
>http://www.roadsideamerica.com/story/2105
>http://floydcollins.tripod.com/
>http://www.cavecity.com/cave_city/floyd_collins.htm
>http://www.americanheritage.com/articles/magazine/ah/1976/6/1976_6_34.shtml

Building a Narrative Essay—no sources

Building an Illustration Essay

>http://findarticles.com/p/articles/mi_m4021/is_2000_Oct/ai_67001162/print?tag=artBody;col1
>http://www.xtrasports1150.com/article.cfm/id/58596
>http://www.factmonster.com/spot/superstitions1.html
>http://www.cbc.ca/sports/columns/top10/superstition.html

75

http://www.docsports.com/sports-superstitions.html
http://www.channelone.com/life/sports/2003/09/17/superstitions/
http://www.infoplease.com/spot/superstitions2.html
http://www.psychologyofsports.com/guest/superstitions2.htm
http://www.dallasnews.com/sharedcontent/dws/spt/basketball/mavs/stories/061106dnsposuperstitions.80efc3e.htmlhttp://www.sptimes.com/2004/08/21/news_pf/Sports/Bad_luck_and_omens_ta.shtml
http://www.mentalfloss.com/blogs/archives/12948
http://forums.sportingnews.com/viewtopic.php?p=241720

Analyzing a Classification Essay—no sources

Building a Classification Essay—no sources

Building a Process Essay—no sources

Analyzing a Comparison/Contrast Essay

http://www.longhairlovers.com/sutherland
http://www.sideshowworld.com/tgod7sutherlands.html
http://www.angelfire.com/art/rapunzellonghair/rapunzellonghairarchive/portrait4.htm

Building a Comparison Contrast Essay

http://www.bollywoodworld.com/whatisbollywood/
http://mutiny.wordpress.com/2007/02/01/bollywood-vs-hollywood-the-complete-breakdown/
http://en.wikipedia.org/wiki/Bollywood

Analyzing a Definition Essay

http://www.digestive.niddk.nih.gov/ddiseases/pubs/celiac/index.htm

Building a Definition Essay—no sources

Building a Persuasion Letter –This is based on an actual incident at an Illinois university.